Prosperity Consciousness

3 Steps to Abundance

Richard Hamlin Yocom

Prosperity Consciousness

3 Steps to Abundance

ISBN 0-9707962-0-X
LCCN 2001093992

Dancing Crow Press

2731 San Carlos Lane
Costa Mesa CA 92626
email: publisher@dancingcrow.com
http://www.dancingcrow.com

Edited by Jim Coleman, Orange, California
Illustrations: Seeker and Cornucopia © by Mona Lisa Lind, Stockholm, Sweden
Illustration: Eagle © Casey Beardan, Newport Beach, CA USA
Photo: Mother holding Child's hand © corbis.com
Cover Design: Richard Yocom
Book Design: Richard Yocom
Book Printed in Garamond type face at CRS Printing, Santa Ana, CA

Prosperity Consciousness

3 Steps to Abundance

Contents

Prosperity Consciousness

Forward

Recently, I was driving home with the car radio tuned to a local news station, KNX, a CBS affiliate. While driving along, one of those little side bars came on called the Osgood File. Charles Osgood was describing the results of a study conducted by Nancy Adler, a Psychology Professor at the University of California at San Francisco. The professor was trying to determine if there might be a relationship between a person's health and feeling of being prosperous. Sure enough, the more prosperous a person believed they were, the better their overall health. Much to her surprise, though, the person's feeling of being prosperous didn't necessarily correspond to actual monetary wealth. For instance, on a scale of one to ten with ten being the highest, an individual might determine their feeling of wealth to be an eight (with a corresponding high health rating) while their actual monetary wealth might only be a four. What a puzzlement!

Metaphysicians have long held that there is a causal relationship between our state of mind and all other areas of our being. This sense of well being discussed on the Osgood File, this state of mind which I call Prosperity Consciousness, comes naturally to some, but for the rest of us, it must be learned. We seek out a guru or scriptures or self help books or a church or some combination of these things. We get on a spiritual path hoping to gain some peace of mind and salvation from ourselves and the negative tapes that play over and over in our minds. We seek to gain that sense of well being described by the professor.

The spiritual path can be as broad as your imagination and encompass all areas of your life. Each area, be it health, relationships, work, hobbies, creative endeavors, prosperity, or whatever, is a perfect reflection of your belief about life. The seeds of growth are present everywhere. We need only be ready to receive their fruit. Many of us start out on this broad highway because of some life changing event or circumstance. Maybe we entered a twelve-step program such as Alcoholics Anonymous, Gamblers Anonymous, or any number of other programs because we found ourselves powerless over circumstances and our lives had become unmanageable. Perhaps we grew up in an abusive household and were introduced to spiritual practices through therapy or some program such as Adult Children of Alcoholics. Maybe it has just been a logical progression of spiritual practices learned as a child in church, synagogue, or temple. Whatever your reason, this book will be of value to you.

It has been said that we are spiritual beings having a human experience. The quality of that experience depends in the main on how well we practice spiritual principles in our daily lives. The subject of prosperity was chosen to introduce some of these principles, because it is something that most everyone can relate to and the results are often quite tangible. Underlying this limited view of what prosperity is, though, is a sense of well being that permeates every aspect of our lives. Prosperity is an area that many people, including the author, have had problems with because we've been taught never to ask for ourselves; that this is a selfish thing to do. However, once we understand that God's will for us is not onerous and can only be good, we begin to see that the concepts laid out here only work to fulfill our destiny as the much-loved children of an all powerful God. We will see that the attitude of prosperity extends well beyond the idea of material wealth and that this attitude encompasses all that would make us happy, joyous and free.

After practicing the simple tasks laid out in this book for a while, you will start to see yourself in a different light. You will see how these principles might be applied to other areas of your life and your personal spiritual path will become a little broader and a little less bumpy.
In my case, The principles helped me to overcome life threatening heart

disease, through the miracle of a heart transplant received in 1995. After having been on my deathbed for many months, I received the call from the hospital letting me know that a compatible heart had been found and that I should proceed to the hospital as quickly as possible. I remember saying to the anesthesiologist, with full faith, as he prepared to put me to sleep: "See you later." Several hours later as I came out of the anesthesia, the first thing I felt was a total peace - as if I were resting in divine hands. The second thing I felt was the rush of life-giving blood through my veins. The pulsations were powerful and I could feel it from the tips of my toes to the top of my head. I was reborn. The whole process from the onset of my illness to the final and complete recuperation was dominated by the knowledge that God had nothing in store for me but good - be that here or in the life hereafter. I hope you too can find this kind of faith which has no boundaries, no beginning and no ending. It is the nature of God to want us to experience a full and satisfying life no matter what our calling might be.

How long do you have to do the things spelled out in this book? Just until they have become ingrained in your consciousness: until they become second nature - a new way of looking at life. Sounds like a long time, doesn't it? Well, you will find that the time flies as you start out on this path and begin to look at things a little differently. The glass will become half full as opposed to half empty. An attitude of skepticism and cynicism will be replaced with an attitude of gratitude. You will find truth in the old adage that grateful people are happy people and those that aren't, aren't. This might take a couple of months, perhaps even a couple of years. Everyone is different. Some of us have a thick layer of old thinking to break through. Don't despair. Just keep at it. The rewards will be yours. Count on it!

I would like to pay special recognition to my artistic collaborators in this endeavor, Mona Lisa Lind of Stockholm, Sweden and Casey Beardan of Newport Beach, California. Their fabulous translation of the concepts in this book to visual images that subtly yet decisively depict the ideas is an amazing demonstration of prosperity. Their efforts result in an experience for the reader/student that is far greater than derived from words alone.

Many people have supported me along my own spiritual path and to some of these I would like to give thanks. First there is my wife, Pam, who supported me during life threatening heart disease and a subsequent heart transplant. Her simple but clear view of life has been and remains an inspiration to me. My children Sharon, Mark, Michael, and Cecilia have imbued me with faith, as I have watched each grow into unique expressions of God's all-powerful love. Then there is my friend of many years, Mary Hardesty-Clayton who introduced me to many of the principles described here and whose endless support and selfless sharing made this work possible. There is also my friend Paul Woodward who has listened to me patiently and with kindness through the years. Then there are my teachers, the Reverend Jim Turrell and Nanielle Devereaux who opened my consciousness to new and expanding ways of viewing life. Finally, thanks to all the wonderful friends and acquaintances I have known over the years, who have helped shape my life and, somehow, have kept me pointed in the right direction. Without their love so freely given, I am convinced I would not be here to share these thoughts with you.

I would like to hear from you with comments and feedback of your demonstrations of prosperity. Please send emails to "ryocom@dancingcrow.com".

Richard H Yocom
July 13, 2001

Prosperity Consciousness

1 *What is Prosperity*

Prosperity is an attitude, a state of mind: To be healthy, happy, and prosperous. One of the greatest Teachers of all told us that "It is done unto you as you believe." In this simple sentence lies the very essence of spiritual truth and the operative word is "as." You are as prosperous as you believe. As your attitude about prosperity grows and expands, so will your demonstration of prosperity. Look at the titles of some of the greatest self help books of all times: "Think and Grow Rich," or "You'll See It When You Believe It," or "You Can Heal Your Life." These all talk about shifts in attitudes. They are about being enthused with Life. They don't talk about being excited. They talk about being enthused. To be enthused means to be filled with the Spirit. Excited means to be stimulated by some external event or thing. Thus, the shift in attitude refers to an inside job that only you can do on yourself. As your attitude changes, your life will follow that shift.

> *So much is a man worth as he esteems himself.*
>
> Francois Rabelais

In this book, tools are presented that can be applied in your everyday life to increase your prosperity consciousness and thus the demonstrations of good in your life. Use these tools for a couple of months on a regular basis and see what happens. After all, if this or any other spiritual practice doesn't work, then why do it? Let's explore a few examples of how these practices have demonstrated in the lives of others:

Mary was a single mother struggling to make ends meet for herself and her three children. She obtained her real estate license and started to practice many of the principles laid out in this book in her business. Within a few years, she became the number one real estate sales person in her community. In fact, her individual sales volume equals or exceeds the combined sales volume of any three other sales people in her town. This was accomplished with a reputation for dedication, competence, integrity, and service. She and her family are living very comfortably today.

Money is the seed of money, and the first guinea is sometimes more difficult to acquire than the second million.

Jean Jacques Rousseau

Paul has been practicing these principles for over twenty years. His demonstrations of prosperity have manifested in several areas including: Abundant good friends from all walks of life; ongoing educational enrichment in the areas of art, psychology, sociology, and metaphysics; a large library of books with topics ranging from current affairs to the classics; and an ever growing sense of peace and contentment. Though not wealthy in monetary terms, his needs have always been met and few would deny that he is a person rich in experiences, knowledge, and creative ideas. Paul has a loving willingness to share his experience, knowledge, and belongings with all. He is indeed a prosperous man.

On a personal note, I became very ill in 1994. Doctors told me that I had end stage heart disease and that my only hope would be to receive a heart transplant. Instead of feeling anger and fear, there was a sense of trust and faith that whatever was to come, it could only be good. Even if I were to pass on to the next life, I knew that all would be well. Over the many months while awaiting a new heart I experienced countless little miracles which reinforced my faith. Finally, the "big" miracle happened and I received the call from the hospital. After awakening from the anesthesia with a newly transplanted heart, I had a tremendous sense of peace. I felt the rush of blood through my body and the strong steady beat of my heart. All was well. I had been given another chance at life. Years of practicing the principles spelled out in this book stood me in good stead.

These are just a few examples that Prosperity Consciousness works. If practiced patiently, it will manifest in our outer world. It is clear that something is going on very deep within our psyche. We have begun to change the way we think about life.

Prosperity Consciousness is a mirror which we hold up to the beliefs of who and what we really are. As our thinking about ourselves changes and grows, the perception of our outer world changes in perfect correlation to our thinking. In this book you will learn to live your way to better thinking by:

◆ recognizing and giving thanks to God for the good which comes into your life;

◆ releasing your good into God's loving care knowing that it is yours because you don't have to have it;

◆ gaining clarity in knowing what you want in life;

◆ asking for your good, living in the expectancy that it shall be "done unto you as you believe;"

◆ sharing your good, knowing that more is on the way pressed down and multiplied.

By practicing these principles in your daily life, your attitude about yourself shifts. You are truly starting to understand and experience the glory of who you are. You begin to see yourself and your relationship to God and to others in a new and wonderfully glorious way. You are beginning to see that you are indeed the much loved child of the Creator of all that is, a loving God you can call your very own.

2 *Recognize Your Good - The First Step*

God is Good and Good is spelled with a capital "G." Good, God: God, Good. They are the same thing. What are the qualities of Good which we can attribute to God? Here are just a few:

Love - Everything, the entire universe, was created by God. In the beginning there was God and nothing; God and no thing else. Thus, all that is created is of God, made out of Its very Self. It is only natural that God would Love Itself, and, in fact, all the Love there is, is of God.

Abundance - If God can think of it, God can create it. There is never any lack in God's creation. Just look at the heavens and believe.

Creativity - God is the creator of all that is. Just look at the immense variety around you. No two people, buds, snowflakes are the very same. Now, that's creative!

Happiness - God looks around at Its creation and is pleased with what It sees. What could bring greater happiness than this?

Beauty - When you looked at the abundant variety around you, you probably noticed the beauty too. Look at the flowers in the spring, the glow of a sunset, the moon on new fallen snow. God is everywhere present and that is where beauty is.

What qualities remind you of God? List four and describe them in two or three sentences. Remember as you do this that God is not complex but very simple. If your definitions seem complex and hard to understand, do them again and again until they are simple and easy to understand.

___

___

___

___

___

___

___

___

___

___

___

We have just made a beginning (and barely a beginning at that) of defining the Good which is of God. As we continue this process we come to the realization that all Good is of God. So what's the problem? Why do we seem to live in a world where there is lack, where there never seems to be enough, when in Truth there is more than enough? God's wonderful feast is laid before us for the taking. We don't have to do anything to earn it. It's ours because we are the much loved children of a Loving God who has created all that is. As we change our perception and start to live a prosperous life, we demonstrate the truth for others to see. The feast is there for them too.

It is now time to start to recognize and to be grateful for the Good that's already in our lives. This is the first step in developing an Attitude of Prosperity.

First do this: Start to recognize and embrace the good in your life. Feel it as the warmth of the sun on your skin or the beauty of new fallen snow. See it in the blossoms of springtime or the wonderful colors of autumn. See it as the smile on the postman's face and the warm hello of a passerby. Smell it in the brisk autumn air or the salty fragrance of the sea. Feel it as the softness of your T shirt or the strength of your new friend's handshake. Sense it in the power of a baseball player's home run or the speed of your favorite football player. God's Good is present everywhere. Just be open to it and you will see it.

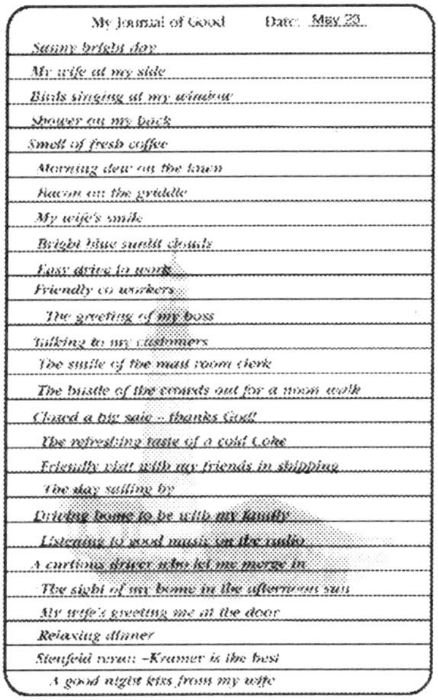
My Journal of Good Date: May 23

Sunny bright day
My wife at my side
Birds singing at my window
Shower on my back
Smell of fresh coffee
Morning dew on the lawn
Bacon on the griddle
My wife's smile
Bright blue sunlit clouds
Easy drive to work
Friendly co workers
The greeting of my boss
Talking to my customers
The smile of the mail room clerk
The bustle of the crowds out for a noon walk
Closed a big sale – thanks God!
The refreshing taste of a cold Coke
Friendly visit with my friends in shipping
The day sailing by
Driving home to be with my family
Listening to good music on the radio
A courteous driver who let me merge in
The sight of my home in the afternoon sun
My wife's greeting me at the door
Relaxing dinner
Seinfeld rerun –Kramer is the best
A good night kiss from my wife

Next do this: Each evening before you go to bed, open this book to the "Journal of Good" in Appendix B and fill one page with the Good that came into your life that day. Start today. (You can use the next page tonight.) You might start with the feel of the warm water on your skin during your morning shower and proceed from there. It won't take long once you get the hang of it, maybe ten to fifteen minutes at most. Do this daily for ninety days. (An additional blank page is available for your use in a separate, downloadable document at the author's web site at www.dancingcrow.com.)

Then do this: Recognize God as the source of your Good and say, "Thank you God for all the Good of this day. I let go of my Good knowing that more is on the way. For this I am grateful."

My Journal of Good Date: ________

You might be wondering, "Well, what do you mean? First you tell me to recognize my good and then to be grateful for it. Now you tell me to let it go. How can this be?"

Remember, God's supply is infinite. There's more there than you can ever imagine. There is enough Good to meet everyones' wants and needs now and for evermore, and then some. If you are not completely filled up, then there is more for you to accept.

The idea of "letting go" is the release of emotional attachment to the Good that comes into our lives and, thus, the release of the need to protect it. It is the ultimate recognition of God as the Source of all Good and it makes room in our consciousness for the receipt of even more Good. Remember this: There is a Power for Good in the Universe, that is greater than yourself. When I thank God for my Good and release it to God's care, I am simply recognizing that God can do a lot better job of running my life than I. So, I think I'll let God do it.

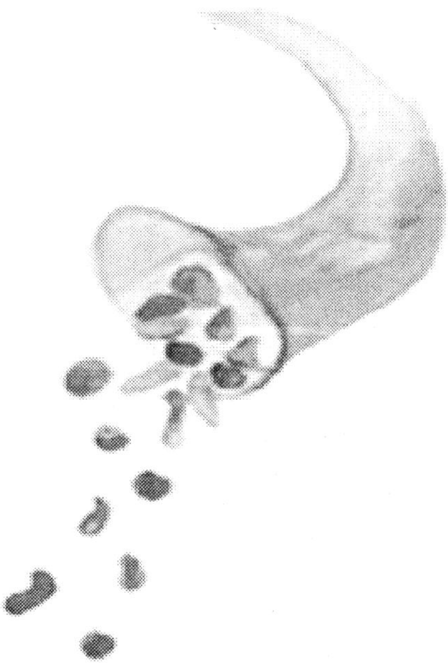

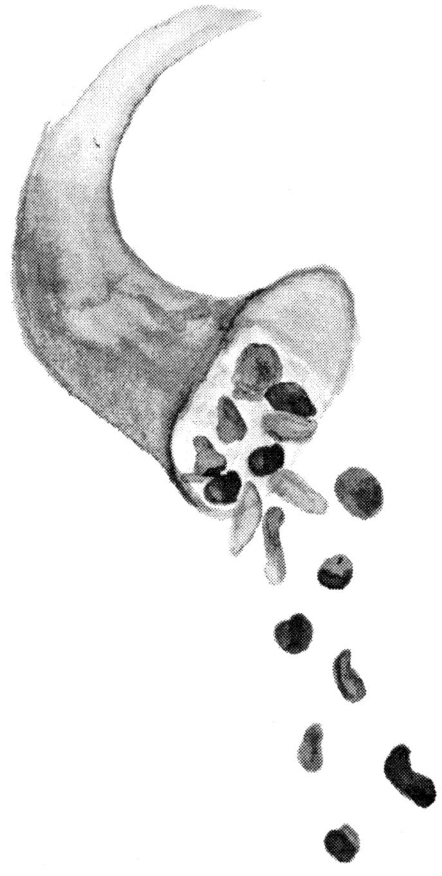

3 *Ask for Your Good - The Second Step*

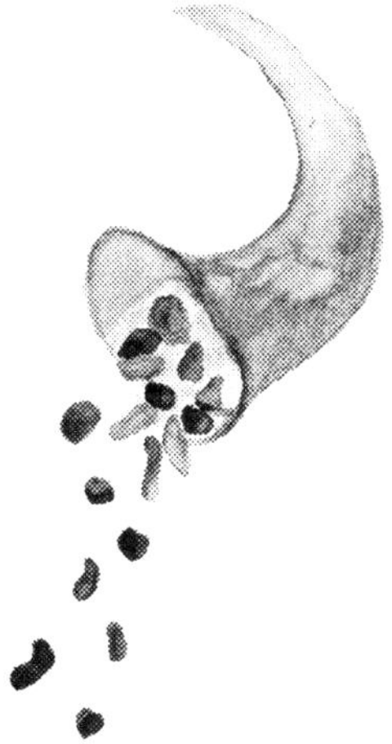

Just ASK. What a concept. Yes, you can do it. You can ask God for what you want and, as long as it doesn't take away from or otherwise hurt another person, it can be yours. There is no reason why you can't have it. Remember that you are building a consciousness of prosperity. As your consciousness expands through regular practice, you provide even more room for the receipt of even greater Good.

You might be thinking: "I can't do that. My whole life I've been taught that I shouldn't pray for myself. That would be a selfish thing to do. Shouldn't I just be praying for guidance in my day-to-day affairs and the courage to cary that out? Shouldn't I be asking for guidance in what I can do for others, not myself?"

Good questions - questions I had to answer for myself, too. As with many other areas of my life, I had to change my attitudes about things and how I react to certain words. After countless hours and days of practicing prayer and meditation I came to understand that God would have nothing in store for me but good. If God is the Father and I am the child, would this not be the case? What father would want it otherwise? I also came to understand that "good" and "prosperity" were synonymous and that prosperity encompassed so much more than material wealth. It encompasses all areas of my life: career, health, home, relationships, travel, everything.

Early on in my spiritual journey I came to see that my difficulties were of my own making and I had to stop blaming others for my problems. Changes in attitude were necessary for me to outwardly demonstrate God's Good in my life. I turned to God to remove my difficulties and I had to start sharing freely what I had found so that others might know and experience this way of life.

Along with this change in my perception of God came a corresponding shift in how I viewed my fellow human beings. If I were the much loved child of a loving Creator, this had to be true of everyone else. If God wanted nothing but Good for me, this had to be true for others, too. We became brothers and sisters, not just in theory but in fact. Also, as I continued to complete my Journal of Good, I got a glimpse of the immensity of God's Good. There was more to go around than could ever be used. Slowly, through the daily practice of spiritual principles, the idea of asking for my good became more and more palatable to me. I was led to read the works of Emmet Fox, Ernest Holmes, Ralph Waldo Emerson, Depaak Chopra and many others. Out of these studies evolved the practices I have laid out here.

How do I ask for my good, you want to know. Well, the best way is to be simple and direct. It doesn't take any magic or trickery. Let's start off by giving an example of how one asks for Good. For example, assume that you want to get a new car - a sparkling new convertible. (It could be anything you desire: a new home, improved health, peace of mind, anything.) Color isn't all that important to you, but because you live in a sunny climate, you'd like to have it light in color, say white or pale blue. You would also like the regular goodies like air conditioning and a stereo cassette/AM/FM Radio. A CD player would also be nice.

To begin, create a mental image of what it is you desire, including how it would feel if it were yours right now, at this very moment. Let's see, we might feel racy, maybe even a bit daring. You would perhaps even feel a bit sexy with the top off and the wind blowing in your hair, as you head to a local department store or take a friend for a ride in the country. You would certainly have a sense of freedom and speed. You could go anywhere you want, when you want. Now, you have the feelings of *Power, Speed, Attraction, and Freedom.* Remember, at the outset of this book, we talked about the qualities we could attribute to God. Think about it for a minute. Aren't these four feelings you could call qualities of God?

> Is not all the Power in the universe that of God's creation? Is any Power greater than God's?
>
> Is there anything in the universe which could make God go at a Speed other than that at which it wishes to go. God will out-picture whatever It wishes, whenever It wishes.
>
> Since God is the Creator of all that is, would not God be able to Attract to Itself all that is needed, when it is needed?
>
> If God has all the Power, Speed, and ability to Attract, doesn't It have all the Freedom necessary to do what It wants, when It wants?

Now, if you combine the physical characteristics of the new car with the feeling you attach to it, you will have what metaphysicians refer to as the "mental equivalent[1]," as stated in the following example:

> *"I have a sense of Speed, Power, Attraction, and Freedom as I ride around town in my wonderful new convertible car."*

Note that you are not thinking in terms of a particular brand of car but simply a "car." This opens up all kinds of possibilities for God to fulfill. It might even be a Lexus or a BMW!

In addition to being specific about what it is you want and the feeling of having it, there is one additional quality of a "mental equivalent." Look at our statement again. Can you tell what it is?

It is the quality of now. It is not some far off in the future, hoped for thing. It is real right now - just as real as your thought about it. So, your mental equivalent is always in the present tense - in the now. In the Spiritual World there is only the eternal now. If you have problems with this concept, ask yourself this simple question: "Is it now yet?"

Now that you have a mental concept of what it is you desire, it's time to frame it in the form of an affirmative prayer[2]. An affirmative prayer is a three step prayer consisting of a declaration, acceptance, and release. It is simple, straight forward, and direct. Again, there is no magic about it.

The three steps in forming the affirmative prayer are as follows:

The Declaration is a restatement of the mental equivalent we just developed.

The Acceptance is a statement accepting our Good, right now, with gratitude and thanksgiving, recognizing God as the source of all Good.

The Release lets the prayer go into the loving care of Spirit to work out the details of how this thing is accomplished and to open us up for the receipt of even more Good into our lives.

Remember that all the Good there is is of God. And God can bring into your reality anything that you desire, as long as it hurts no one and takes from no one. For instance, in our mental equivalent for the convertible, we didn't ask for John's car or Sally's car for this would be the same thing as envy or jealousy. Instead, you asked for a car that produced the qualities and feelings you desire. So, let's form our prayer:

> "Dear God, Creator of all that is, right now, I declare for myself, a wonderful new convertible which provides me with all the freedom, power and speed I could imagine in a package which attracts to me even more of God's Good. Thank you God for the wonderful reality of this new car. I accept it into my life right now with a sense of joy and thanksgiving. I let go of this prayer totally and completely into the care of Loving Spirit knowing, that as I do so, it is done.
>
> And so it is."

Note that this prayer is very specific about what qualities you want and how you would feel if you had it. In no way do you tell God how to do it. That's up to Spirit to work out. It is our job to live our lives one day at a time, doing what's in front of us with an attitude of love and service. The results are up to God.

> *Great men are they who see that spiritual is stronger than any material force, that thoughts rule the world.*
>
> Ralph Waldo Emerson

And now you just might be saying to yourself: "Is this for real."

This stuff is for the weak. I'm supposed to make these things happen in my own life, not depend on God or anyone to help me get what I want. If I don't assert myself, I can't possibly have what I want." Or you might be thinking that you can't possibly have that car because you don't have the money in the bank. Such are the arguments that our past experiences, conditioning and belief systems play in our head. These statements seem logical and they may even be based on fact. For instance, our school system fosters the idea that we are to be independent people, responsible for making things happen in our own lives. Indeed, we may not have enough money right now in our checking account to go out and buy a new car. Just remember, these may be facts but they are not the Truth. The Truth is that we are responsible for our thinking, our attitudes, and our actions. God is responsible for the results. It is done unto you as you believe.

When our ego bursts in and thoughts like these occur, just listen to them for a few minutes, recognize what it is, then ask it: "God can't do what?" And have a good laugh. If this occurs on a regular basis, make a simple change to your prayer which denies any power to such thoughts and replaces them with a statement of the Truth. Your prayer might now read as follows:

> "Dear God, creator of all that is, right now, I declare for myself, a wonderful new convertible, which provides me with all the freedom, power and speed I could imagine in a package which attracts to me even more of God's Good. *There is no power in any thought of lack of enough money. God is the source of all Good and knows of absolutely no lack. All Good is of God and is mine to use in the creation of my own Good.* Thank you God for the wonderful reality of this wonderful new car. I accept it into my life right now with a sense of joy and thanksgiving. I let go of this prayer totally and completely into the care of Loving Spirit knowing that as I do so, it is done.
>
> And so it is."

> *Every good gift and every perfect gift is from above*
>
> The General Epistle of James, 1:1

For the third time, when we say release the prayer, we do mean let it go. Learn to live each day in the expectancy of Good, without figuring out how it should look or how it should be. Don't have expectations that this or that will happen in a certain, specific way. Expectations get us in trouble because they try to tell God how to do God's business. It's our business to ask. It's God's business to work out the how and when it will be brought about.

For those of you still skeptical, let's see how this compares to the thought process and actions followed by my friend, Jim, as he was planning for his retirement. One of the things Jim was considering for his retirement was the acquisition of a home at Lake Tahoe. Here are some of the things he was looking for in this property. He wanted a yard where he could tinker. He wanted the house to be in a quiet neighborhood. It should be reasonably close to the lake with a view of the lake. These thoughts amounted to a mental equivalent of the property even though Jim didn't know he was doing such a thing.

As the time for Jim's retirement came closer, he made a trip to Tahoe to look at property. After spending Saturday and a part of Sunday looking at houses, he had not found the right one for him. In his musings he said to himself, "God's will not mine be done." As he was driving through South Lake Tahoe he passed a realty office and noticed a car parked in front. In a moment of inspiration he decided to stop and go into to see what might be available in this locale. The very first home he was shown had all the attributes that were important to him. Not only that, the house was reasonably priced! Within just a matter of days, offers were exchanged and the house was his. In this brief scenario lies all of the elements of what comprises our affirmative prayer, just not formally.

After they write their prayers, some people put them in a brown paper bag which they put in the freezer. Others have a shoe box or cigar box in which they place their prayers. Still others do them on their computer and tuck them away in a safe folder. They refer to these as their "God Box." After some period of time, say six months or a year, you can refer back to your prayers to see what has demonstrated in your life. You will be delighted with what has come your way. In many cases it will even exceed that for which you asked.

So, let's take a minute and construct a prayer of our own. Is there anything you have been wishing for or would really like to have or do? How does it appear in your mind's eye? What would it feel like if you had it right now? Contemplate this then write down a description of what it is you want in as much detail as possible. Then write your mental equivalent.

*What I Want:*____

____

Mental Equivalent:

Ok, now, lets construct our prayer. Remember, there are three parts: (1) declaration, (2) acceptance with thanksgiving, and (3) release. If you wish, after your declaration you may add a statement denying any blocks that come up followed by an affirmation of the Truth about God. Review the convertible example, if necessary.

My First Affirmative Prayer

Declaration: Dear God, Creator of all that is

Denial:

Statement of Truth:

Acceptance with thanksgiving:

Release: ____

____

____

____

Amen

So, there you have it. That's all you need to do to ask for your Good. This basic format of a prayer is all that is needed to meet your needs whether your area of interest be relationships, health, career, or whatever. When you are confronted with an apparent problem, take a moment before you act and form in your mind a brief prayer requesting clarity. The answer will come.

---

1) See "Mental Equivalent" by Emmet Fox, Unity Books, Unity School of Christianity, 1901 NW Blue Parkway, Unity Village, MO 64065-0001

2) The prayer format is based on the Spiritual Mind Treatment prayer format developed by Holmes, Ernest, 1938/1966,"The Science of Mind", 50th Anniversary Edition, NY: G.P. Putnam's Sons. The Spiritual Mind Treatment adds two steps to the three step format presented in "Prosperity Consciousness". The two steps precede the declaration step and are "recognition" and "unification." Recognition is a statement of the Truth about God (eg. "Dear God, Creator of all that Is,"). Unification is a statement affirming our oneness with God (eg. "I am created by God out of It's Very Stuff.").

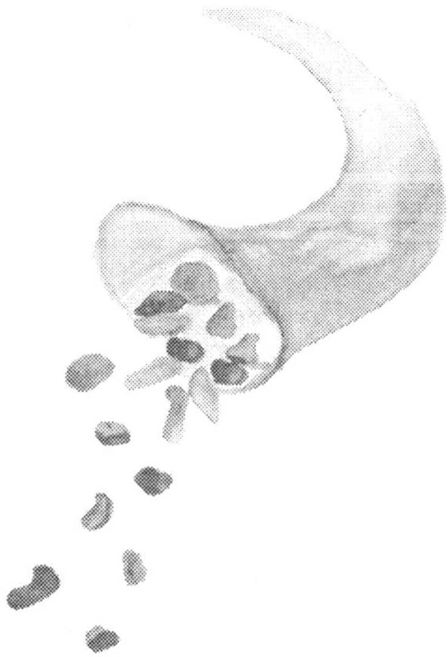

4 *Circulate Your Good - The Third Step*

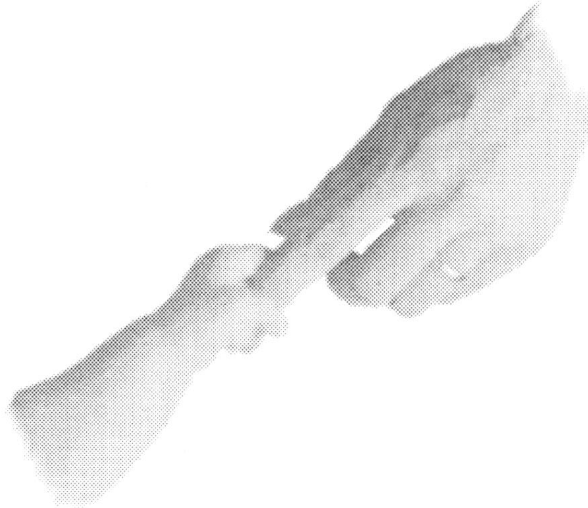

So far, we have focused on the thinking processes of prosperity and not a lot about action. Once we have said our prayer or prayers, what do we do then? Very simply, we go about our daily business, whatever that might be, and try to be of maximum service in whatever it is we are doing. If we are at work for instance, we are attentive and involved in our daily assignments, for in being of service to others we are serving the universe. We are, in the best sense, being of maximum service to ourselves. At the same time, we are alert for opportunities to be helpful to co-workers and supervisors. If an opportunity presents itself, we gladly take the ball and run with it.

If possible, we find things we can do for others anonymously - where we don't take credit for a good deed. This recognizes at the deepest possible level that God is the source of all Good and that we are really the instrument and God is the source. As an example, assume that your friend, Mary's husband, has been very ill and Mary hasn't been able to afford to go to the movies for a long time. The next time you're at the theater, buy her a pass and place it where she's sure to find it, like in her mail box or in a door jam. I know of one woman who, when in the super market, will place a couple of dollars between bags of rice knowing that whomever finds them will be able to use the money. Don't tell anyone you did this - it's a secret between you and God. Giving Good pays big dividends and "as you give, you receive."

Can you think of examples of things which you can do anonymously? List them here : ______________________________

____

____

____

____

____

____

____

It is in taking such action that you are allowing Spirit to move through you in an expression of Good. You are are creating a channel for even more Good to come into your life. God always has a tendency to give back that which has been freely given and It will do so in the most unexpected ways, "pressed down and multiplied."

An important spiritual principal known to all ages is that of tithing. This is the act of supporting that organization or body of work which supports you spiritually. Tithing recognizes God as the source of all Good and gives back to the Universe a portion of that which God has given you. By portion, we mean some percentage of your income, whether that be your weekly allowance or monthly pay check. In ancient times, the expected tithe was ten per cent of wages. For our purpose you can choose any percentage you feel comfortable with. I know people who tithe five per cent and I know others who tithe as much as one third of their income. I know one who not only tithes 30 per cent but has found other ways to tithe even more, such as by giving his estate over to charitable organizations for fund raising events. The universe has rewarded him well for the company he started some fifty years ago in his garage is now one of the largest companies in the world.

Men grind and grind in the mill of a truism, and nothing comes out but what was put in. But the moment they desert the tradition for a spontaneous thought, then poetry, wit, hope, virtue, learning, anecdote, all flock to their aid."

Ralph Waldo Emerson

So, what's the point? Well, what we have done is set into motion the law of circulation, which recognizes money as a physical out-picturing of God's Good as a means of placing value on that which we acquire, be it goods or services. By keeping money flowing in the creation of God's Good, we are building in our own consciousness even more space for prosperity to demonstrate for us and those we love. Our attitude of prosperity is enhanced, we are served, and the universe is served.

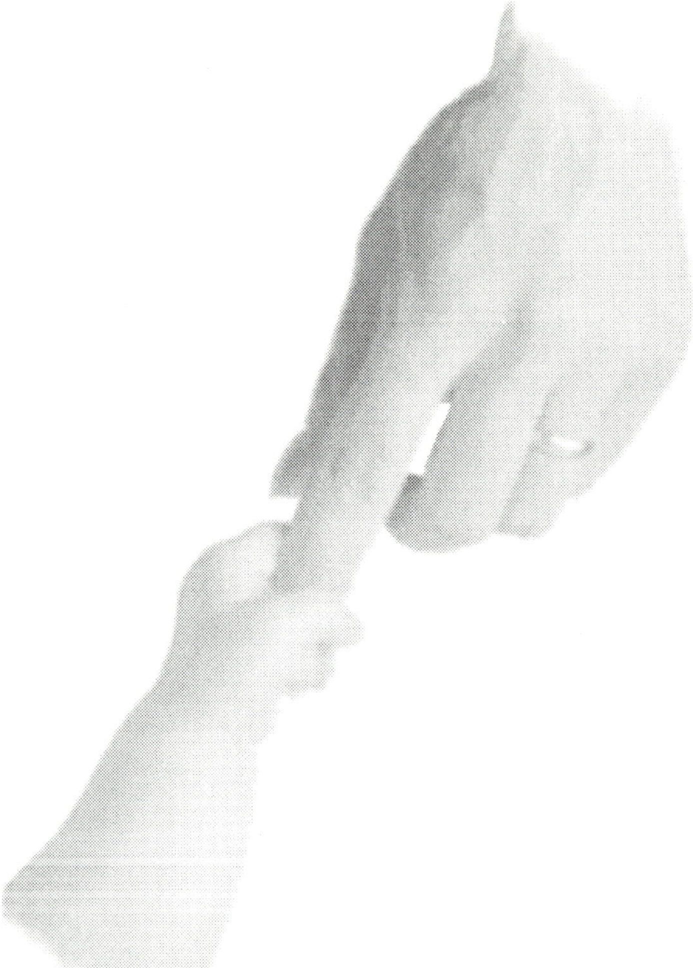

5 *A Plan for Life*

Now you have the hang of it. Just suppose for a moment that you could apply these same principles to any area of your life. If they can work for prosperity, why not my relationships and my career? Why not where I live and the things I do with my leisure time? How about creative endeavors like painting and sculpture? Why not?

Good questions. You're right. These principles can be successfully applied in all areas of your life. If you continue the process started in Chapter Two of listing all the good characteristics you can attribute to God, you will see that they also apply to you and any area of your life you may be contemplating. The principles are based on one simple premise: God is all things! Simple yet profound. God is not separate and apart from you. God is right here and right now and is eager to lay the feast before you. Nothing pleases the Creator more than your happiness, joy and freedom. So prepare yourself to look up and beyond your old limited perception of yourself and prepare for a ride beyond your wildest dreams.

During the coming months, as your thoughts turn to the various areas of your life, contemplate the nature of God and prepare your own personal prayers of affirmation. Use the prayer forms provided in Appendix A to develop a mental equivalent of how you want to experience your Good, just as you did with prosperity. Then develop your prayer. Once you have practiced it a little, it will become second nature but don't become complacent. Writing it down forces clarity of thought and clarity is required for bountiful results.

Use "Appendix B" as your Journal of Good. Watch all the Good which comes into your life on a daily basis. As you do this you will come to realize that your Good can come from anywhere and usually does. Don't expect that your Good must come from this place or that person. It comes from anywhere. Be open to it, aware of it, and receptive. If you're like me, you will wonder how much you've missed because you lived your life with blinders on. My expectations that Good must come from this source or that only served to limit God's Good in my life and God knows no limits. So, drop your expectations which serve only to limit you. Live instead with with the expectancy of Good. God: Good, they are interchangeable, one in the same.

Summary

Prosperity is more attitude than anything else. It is a state of mind dominated by a sense of well being - a sense of abundance which is built up over time through practice.

The first step in developing this attitude is recognizing all the good that comes into our lives on a daily basis. We do this by:

◆ Completing daily a page in our "Journal of Good;"

◆ Thanking God for that Good;

◆ Letting go of the Good so we have room for more.

The second step in the development of our attitude of prosperity is asking for our good. This is done through the use of an affirmative prayer which has three steps:

◆ Declaring our good right now in the form of a "mental equivalent" which specifically describes the qualities of what we want and how we will feel when we have it.

◆ Accepting that Good with thanksgiving.

◆ Releasing our prayer into God's care with the expectancy that God will work out the details of how we are to receive our Good.

It has been said that "faith without works is dead." It's up to us now to do the footwork in step three so God can move in our lives. This is accomplished through the Law of Reciprocity which states that "As you sow, so shall you reap." This law is set into motion for your Good by:

◆ Doing what is front of you to the very best of your ability.

◆ Being of Love and Service to those around you, and, on a daily basis, choosing one good deed you can do anonymously..

◆ Keeping the Good flowing through your tithes and gifts.

This stuff works! Take the time and prove it to yourself. The more you demonstrate Good the more you will live in the expectancy of Good with an attitude of prosperity.

In Closing, the following quote from Marianne Williamson's book "A Return to Love" and used in Nelson Mandella's 1994 Inaugural Speech as the President of South Africa summarizes what we have been talking about in these pages:

"Our deepest fear is not that we are inadequate.
Our deepest fear is that we are powerful beyond measure.

It is our light, not our darkness, that most frightens us.

We ask ourselves
'Who am I to be brilliant, gorgeous, talented and fabulous?'

Actually, who are you not to be?

You are a child of God.

Your playing small doesn't serve the world.
There is nothing enlightened about shrinking so that other people won't feel insecure around you.

We are born to make manifest the glory of God
that is within us.

It's not just in some of us; it's in everyone.

And so, as we let our own light shine, we unconsciously give other people permission to do the same.

As we are liberated from our own fear,
our presence automatically liberates others."

You have entered a broad highway which, if followed, will transform your Life through "Prosperity Consciousness." Like the eagle, prepare to soar ever higher as you practice these principles in your daily lives.

Appendix A

Affirmative Prayer

Affirmative Prayer -- Date ______

What I want: ______

Mental Equivelant: ______

The Prayer

Declaration: *Dear God, Creator of all that is*

Denial:

Statement of Truth:

Acceptance with Thanksgiving:

Release:

Affirmative Prayer -- Date ______

What I want: ______

Mental Equivelant: ______

The Prayer

Declaration: Dear God, Creator of all that is

Denial:

Statement of Truth:

Acceptance with Thanksgiving:

Release:

Affirmative Prayer -- Date ______

What I want: ______

Mental Equivelant: ______

The Prayer

Declaration: ***Dear God, Creator of all that is***

Denial:

Statement of Truth:

Acceptance with Thanksgiving:

Release:

Affirmative Prayer -- Date ______

What I want: ______

Mental Equivelant: ______

The Prayer

Declaration: Dear God, Creator of all that is

Denial:

Statement of Truth:

Acceptance with Thanksgiving:

Release:

Affirmative Prayer -- Date ______

What I want: ______

Mental Equivelant: ______

The Prayer

Declaration: *Dear God, Creator of all that is*

Denial:

Statement of Truth:

Acceptance with Thanksgiving:

Release:

Affirmative Prayer -- Date ______

What I want: ______________________________

Mental Equivelant: ______________________________

The Prayer

Declaration: *Dear God, Creator of all that is*

Denial:

Statement of Truth:

Acceptance with Thanksgiving:

Release:

Affirmative Prayer -- Date ______

What I want: ______

Mental Equivelant: ______

The Prayer

Declaration: Dear God, Creator of all that is

Denial:

Statement of Truth:

Acceptance with Thanksgiving:

Release:

Affirmative Prayer -- Date ______

What I want: ______

Mental Equivelant: ______

The Prayer

Declaration: *Dear God, Creator of all that is*

Denial:

Statement of Truth:

Acceptance with Thanksgiving:

Release:

Affirmative Prayer -- Date ______

What I want: ______

Mental Equivelant: ______

The Prayer

Declaration: *Dear God, Creator of all that is* ____________

Denial: ____________

Statement of Truth: ____________

Acceptance with Thanksgiving: ____________

Release: ____________

Affirmative Prayer -- Date ______

What I want: ______________________________

Mental Equivelant: ______________________________

The Prayer

Declaration: Dear God, Creator of all that is

Denial:

Statement of Truth:

Acceptance with Thanksgiving:

Release:

Affirmative Prayer -- Date ______

What I want: ______

Mental Equivelant: ______

The Prayer

Declaration: *Dear God, Creator of all that is*

Denial:

Statement of Truth:

Acceptance with Thanksgiving:

Release:

Affirmative Prayer -- Date ______

What I want: ______

Mental Equivelant: ______

The Prayer

Declaration: *Dear God, Creator of all that is*

Denial:

Statement of Truth:

Acceptance with Thanksgiving:

Release:

Affirmative Prayer -- Date ______

What I want: ______

Mental Equivelant: ______

The Prayer

Declaration: Dear God, Creator of all that is

Denial:

Statement of Truth:

Acceptance with Thanksgiving:

Release:

Affirmative Prayer -- Date ______

What I want: ____________________

Mental Equivelant: ____________________

The Prayer

Declaration: Dear God, Creator of all that is

Denial:

Statement of Truth:

Acceptance with Thanksgiving:

Release:

Affirmative Prayer -- Date ______

What I want: ______

Mental Equivelant: ______

The Prayer

Declaration: Dear God, Creator of all that is

Denial:

Statement of Truth:

Acceptance with Thanksgiving:

Release:

Affirmative Prayer -- Date ______

What I want: ______

Mental Equivelant: ______

The Prayer

Declaration: Dear God, Creator of all that is

Denial:

Statement of Truth:

Acceptance with Thanksgiving:

Release:

Affirmative Prayer -- Date ______

What I want: ______

Mental Equivelant: ______

The Prayer

Declaration: *Dear God, Creator of all that is*

Denial:

Statement of Truth:

Acceptance with Thanksgiving:

Release:

Affirmative Prayer -- Date ______

What I want: ______

Mental Equivelant: ______

The Prayer

Declaration: Dear God, Creator of all that is

Denial:

Statement of Truth:

Acceptance with Thanksgiving:

Release:

Affirmative Prayer -- Date ______

What I want: ______________________________

____

____

____

____

____

____

____

____

____

____

____

Mental Equivelant: ______________________________

____

____

____

____

____

____

____

____

____

____

____

____

The Prayer

Declaration: Dear God, Creator of all that is

Denial:

Statement of Truth:

Acceptance with Thanksgiving:

Release:

Affirmative Prayer -- Date ______

What I want: ______

Mental Equivelant: ______

The Prayer

Declaration: Dear God, Creator of all that is

Denial:

Statement of Truth:

Acceptance with Thanksgiving:

Release:

Appendix B

Journal of Good

My Journal of Good Date: ________

My Journal of Good Date: ________

My Journal of Good Date: ________

My Journal of Good Date: ________

My Journal of Good Date: ________

My Journal of Good   Date: ________

My Journal of Good Date: ________

My Journal of Good Date: ________

My Journal of Good Date: ________

My Journal of Good Date: ________

My Journal of Good Date: ________

My Journal of Good Date: ________

My Journal of Good Date: ________

My Journal of Good Date: ________

My Journal of Good Date: ________

My Journal of Good Date: ________

My Journal of Good Date: ________

My Journal of Good Date: ________

My Journal of Good   Date: ________

My Journal of Good Date: ________

My Journal of Good Date: ________

My Journal of Good Date: ________

My Journal of Good Date: ________

My Journal of Good Date: ________

My Journal of Good Date: ________

My Journal of Good Date: ________

My Journal of Good Date: ________

My Journal of Good Date: ________

My Journal of Good Date: ________

My Journal of Good Date: ________

My Journal of Good Date: ________

My Journal of Good Date: ________

My Journal of Good Date: ________

My Journal of Good Date: ______

My Journal of Good Date: ________

My Journal of Good Date: ________

My Journal of Good Date: ________

My Journal of Good Date: ________

My Journal of Good Date: ________

My Journal of Good Date: ________

My Journal of Good Date: ________

My Journal of Good Date: ________

My Journal of Good Date: ________

My Journal of Good Date: ______

My Journal of Good Date: ________

My Journal of Good Date: ________

My Journal of Good Date: ________

My Journal of Good Date: ________

My Journal of Good Date: ________

My Journal of Good Date: ________

My Journal of Good Date: ________

My Journal of Good Date: ________

My Journal of Good Date: ________

My Journal of Good Date: ________

My Journal of Good Date: ________

My Journal of Good Date: ________

My Journal of Good Date: ________

My Journal of Good Date: ________

My Journal of Good Date: ________

My Journal of Good Date: ________

My Journal of Good Date: ________

My Journal of Good Date: ________

My Journal of Good Date: ________

My Journal of Good Date: ________

My Journal of Good Date: ________

My Journal of Good Date: ________

My Journal of Good Date: ________

My Journal of Good Date: ________

My Journal of Good Date: ________

My Journal of Good Date: ________

My Journal of Good Date: ________

My Journal of Good   Date: ________

My Journal of Good Date: ________

My Journal of Good Date: ________

My Journal of Good Date: ________

My Journal of Good Date: ________

My Journal of Good Date: ________

My Journal of Good Date: ________

My Journal of Good Date: ________

My Journal of Good Date: ________

My Journal of Good Date: ________

My Journal of Good Date: ________

My Journal of Good Date: ________

My Journal of Good Date: ______

My Journal of Good Date: ________

My Journal of Good Date: ________

My Journal of Good Date: ________

Order Form (Free Delivery in USA)

To order "Prosperity Consciousness" from the publisher, complete this form and send it either by mail or fax. (Allow 1 to 2 weeks for delivery.)

Fax Number: (714) 429-1510

Mailing Address:
Dancing Crow Press
2731 San Carlos Lane
Costa Mesa, CA 92626 USA

Order Info:

Quantity ordered _____ X $16.95 = $_________

(California Residents add 7.5% tax) = _________

Total Cost ——————$_________

Your name __________________ Date ________

Delivery Instructions: Mail to

Name ______________________________________

Address Line One ____________________________

Address Line two ____________________________

City __________________ State ____ Zip ________

Telephone _______-_______-______________

Payment Instructions:
Check or Money Order Enclosed: ___
(Make payable to: "Dancing Crow Press")
Visa __ M/C___ Amex ___ Discover ___

Card Number: _________________ Exp date ___/___
MO / YR

Name as appears on card _______________________

Signature: ____________________________